Dutch Oven
DESSERT
Cookbook

By
Carla Randolph

CFI
Springville, Utah

ISBN 13: 978-1-59955-123-4

Published by CFI, an imprint of Cedar Fort, Inc., 2373 W. 700 S., Springville, UT, 84663
Distributed by Cedar Fort, Inc., www.cedarfort.com

LIBRARY OF CONGRESS CATALOGING-IN-PUBLICATION DATA

Randolph, Carla.
  Dutch oven desserts / Carla Randolph.
    p. cm.
  ISBN 978-1-59955-123-4
  1. Dutch oven cookery. 2. Desserts. I. Title.

  TX840.D88R364 2008
  641.8'6—dc22

                        2007045105

Cover design by Jeremy Beal
Cover design © 2008 by Lyle Mortimer
Edited and typeset by Annaliese B. Cox

Printed in the United States of America

10 9 8 7 6 5 4 3 2 1

Printed on acid-free paper

CONTENTS

ACKNOWLEDGMENTS

I'd like to thank my parents for raising me to enjoy the great out-of-doors and for their encouragement and support in cooking Dutch. Also, thanks to my three boys for eagerly sampling the many recipes that I have tried through the years. And many thanks to Lee Nelson for hiring me sight unseen to cook on his Adventure Trail Rides. He has been a great friend and support in putting this cookbook together.

INTRODUCTION

These recipes can all be baked in a regular oven in your home or RV. Usually a 9x13 baking pan is sufficient. All recipes have the oven temperature given in parentheses. To convert these temperatures to use with Dutch ovens, please follow the temperature conversion chart. Remember to use the chart's recommended number of briquettes for top and bottom heat.

I always line my Dutch ovens with heavy-duty aluminum foil, especially on dusty trails and camp outs. This is because there is often very little water for cleanup. Also, the foil helps keep sand from mixing in with the food. The foil make its easier to clean the Dutch oven, especially when using sugar and egg in these recipes.

TEMPERATURE CONVERSION CHART

	350°F	375°F	400°F	425°F
10-inch Dutch Oven				
Total Briquettes	21	23	25	27
Briquettes on Top/Bottom	14/7	16/7	17/8	18/9
12-inch				
Total Briquettes	25	27	29	31
Top/Bottom	17/8	18/9	19/10	21/10
14-inch				
Total Briquettes	32	34	36	38
Top/Bottom	21/11	22/12	24/12	25/13

Do not preheat the Dutch oven. As you cook, make sure the lid is *on* unless otherwise specified. Have two-thirds heat on top, one-third heat on bottom. To bake in an indoor oven, use the temperatures in parentheses at the end of each recipe.

COBBLERS & CRISPS

In the olden days, cobblers were also called grunts, slumps, and spoon pies. Today, cobblers and crisps are still a favorite Dutch oven dessert. The flavors are endless—limited only by your creativity. They can be made from fresh, frozen, canned, or bottled fruit. The toppings on cobblers and crisps can be as varied as the people who enjoy them. Cobblers and crisps are fun "first timer" Dutch oven dishes. Simple to make—but, oh so good!

Listed in this section are several tried and true cobbler and crisp recipes, along with some that may not be too common. Also included are several crust recipes that will be fun to try out. All these recipes can be served hot from the oven with a variety of sweet, creamy toppings.

The recipes in this section should be cooked in a 12-inch Dutch oven unless otherwise noted. Each recipe includes the temperature for a conventional oven and can be baked in a 9x13 baking dish.

Crust Toppings for Cobblers and Crisps

Try any of these methods for making crusts. Use any flavor of cake mix that complements the fruit filling. See list below for recommended combinations.

Crumbly

Sprinkle dry cake mix over fruit filling. Pour 1 cube melted butter over cake mix.

Cakey

Prepare cake mix as instructed on package and pour over fruit filling.

Crunchy

Combine 2 cups oatmeal, 1 cube melted butter, and 1 dry cake mix. Sprinkle over top of fruit filling.

Crispy

Mix together 1 cube softened butter, 1 cup flour, 1 cup oatmeal, and ½ cup brown sugar until mixture resembles coarse crumbs. Sprinkle over top of fruit.

Cake Mix and Fruit Filling Combinations

yellow cake mix—any fruit filling
white cake mix—any fruit filling
chocolate cake mix—cherry filling
orange cake mix—blueberry filling
spice cake mix—peach filling
lemon cake mix—blueberry filling

Tip: Don't forget to drizzle these creamy toppings over any cobbler or crisp: frozen whipped topping, ice cream, heavy unsweetened cream.

Basic & Easy Fruit Cobblers

1–2 (21 oz. each) cans cherry, peach, or blueberry pie filling
1 (18¼ oz.) box yellow or white dry cake mix
1 cube butter, melted

Empty pie filling into 12-inch Dutch oven. Sprinkle dry cake mix over top of filling. Do not stir! Drizzle melted butter over dry cake mix. Cover and bake using top and bottom heat for 20–25 minutes or until topping is crisp and fruit is hot and bubbly. Serve with your favorite cream topping. (375°F)

Apple Crisp

2–3 (21 oz. each) cans apple slices, undrained
3–4 tsp. cinnamon
1 (18¼ oz.) box dry cake mix
1 cube butter, melted

Pour undrained apples into Dutch oven and stir in cinnamon. Sprinkle dry cake mix over top of filling. Do not stir! Drizzle melted butter over dry cake mix. Cover and bake using top and bottom heat for 20–25 minutes or until topping is crisp and fruit is hot and bubbly. Serve with your favorite cream topping. (375°F)

Apple-Ginger Dessert

2 cans applesauce
1 box gingerbread mix
2 c. water

In a foil-lined Dutch oven, pour in applesauce and heat over about 10 briquettes. Heat until bubbly. Meanwhile, combine gingerbread mix and water. Remove oven from coals. Pour gingerbread over applesauce and spread evenly. Do not stir. Cover and put oven over 5 briquettes, with about 20 on top. Bake 40 minutes or until knife inserted in center comes out clean. Serve with whipped topping. (375°F)

Apple Pandowdy

4 tart apples, peeled, cored, and sliced
¾ tsp. cinnamon
½ c. molasses
5 Tbsp. butter, divided
2⅓ c. biscuit mix
½ c. milk
3 Tbsp. sugar
garnish: whipped topping, nutmeg

Place sliced apples in a 10-inch Dutch oven; sprinkle with cinnamon. Drizzle molasses over cinnamon and dot with 2 tablespoons butter. Stir together biscuit mix, milk, and sugar. Melt remaining butter and blend into biscuit mixture. Knead dough 10 times and roll out to ½-inch thick. Lay dough over apple mixture and cut steam vents. Cover and bake using top and bottom heat for about 30 minutes. Spoon into bowls and garnish with whipped topping and nutmeg. (375°F)

Nutty Apple Crisp

1 cube butter, melted
1 c. brown sugar
½ c. apple juice
½ c. flour
¼ tsp. salt
½ tsp. baking powder
1 tsp. cinnamon
¼ tsp. mace
1 c. oatmeal
½ c. wheat germ
½ c. chopped pecans
1 c. peeled, cored, and
  diced apples

Stir together butter and brown sugar by hand until well blended. Stir in juice, flour, salt, baking powder, cinnamon, and mace; blend well. Add oatmeal, wheat germ, and pecans; stir until blended. Gently fold in apples. Spread in a greased, foil-lined 10-inch Dutch oven. Cover and bake using top and bottom heat for 30 minutes or until the top is browned and crisp. (350°F)

Crunchy Oat & Fruit Crisp

1 c. oatmeal
¾ c. brown sugar, divided
5 Tbsp. flour, divided
⅓ c. butter, melted
1 c. fresh or frozen
  blueberries
1 c. fresh or frozen
  cherries
4 apples, peeled, cored,
  and thickly sliced
¼ c. orange juice
  concentrate
1 Tbsp. cinnamon

Mix together oatmeal, ½ cup brown sugar, 2 tablespoons flour, and butter; set aside. In a separate bowl, combine remaining ingredients. Stir until fruit is evenly coated. Spoon filling into a greased, foil-lined 10-inch Dutch oven. Sprinkle topping over filling. Cover and bake using top and bottom heat for 30–35 minutes or until apples are tender and topping is brown. (350°F)

Caramel Apple Crisp

½ c. flour
½ c. sugar
½ tsp. cinnamon
¼ tsp. nutmeg
40 caramels, quartered
9 c. peeled, sliced baking
    apples
¼ c. orange juice

Topping
½ c. sugar
⅓ c. flour
3 Tbsp. butter
⅔ c. quick-cooking
    oatmeal
½ c. chopped walnuts

Combine flour, sugar, cinnamon, and nutmeg; add caramels and stir to coat. In a separate bowl, toss apples with orange juice. Stir in caramel mixture and spread into a greased 12-inch Dutch oven.

To make topping, combine sugar and flour in a small bowl; cut in butter until crumbly. Add oatmeal and walnuts; then sprinkle over apples. Cover and bake using top and bottom heat for 30–40 minutes or until apples are tender. (350°F)

Last Chance Apple Crisp

4 c. peeled, cored, and
    cubed apples
1¼ c. brown sugar,
    divided
¼ c. water
2 tsp. cinnamon
1 c. flour
1 tsp. salt
⅓ c. butter, melted

Place apples in a greased 10-inch Dutch oven. Add ¾ cup brown sugar, water, and cinnamon. In a large bowl, blend together flour, remaining brown sugar, salt, and butter to make crumbs. Spread crumbs evenly over apples. Cover and bake using top and bottom heat for about 50 minutes. Serve with cream poured over each serving. (350°F)

Cran-Apple Crunch

1 c. sugar
1 c. water
2 c. cranberries
2 c. peeled, cored, and
    chopped tart apples
1 c. quick-cooking
    oatmeal
½ c. brown sugar
⅓ c. flour
½ tsp. salt
¼ c. butter
½ c. chopped nuts

Place sugar and water in a saucepan; boil for 5 minutes. Add cranberries; heat another 5 minutes. Remove from heat; stir in apples. Pour into a greased 10-inch Dutch oven; set aside. Mix oatmeal, brown sugar, flour, and salt together; cut in butter until mixture resembles coarse crumbs. Sprinkle over cranberry mixture; then sprinkle nuts on top. Cover and bake using top and bottom heat for about 35 minutes. (350°F)

Clear Creek Apple Crunch

4 c. peeled, cored, and
    cubed apples
1 c. sugar
1 tsp. cinnamon
1 tsp. nutmeg
1 c. butter, divided
1 c. flour
¾ c. brown sugar

Place apples in the bottom of a greased 12-inch Dutch oven. Sprinkle with sugar, cinnamon, and nutmeg; dot generously with ½ cup butter. In a separate bowl, mix flour and brown sugar together; cut in remaining butter until mixture resembles coarse crumbs. Sprinkle over fruit. Cover and bake using top and bottom heat for about 20 minutes. (350°F)

Apple Pecan Cobbler

4 c. apples, thinly sliced
1½ c. sugar, divided
½ tsp. cinnamon
¾ c. chopped pecans, divided
1 c. flour
1 tsp. baking powder
1 tsp. salt
1 egg, beaten
½ c. evaporated milk
⅓ c. butter, melted

Arrange apple slices in an even layer in the bottom of a greased 12-inch Dutch oven. Mix together ½ cup sugar, cinnamon, and ½ cup pecans in a small bowl; sprinkle mixture over apples. In a separate bowl, sift together flour, remaining sugar, baking powder, and salt; set aside. In a separate bowl, whisk together egg, evaporated milk, and butter; add to flour mixture all at once. Stir until smooth. Pour mixture over apples and sprinkle top with remaining pecans. Cover and bake using top and bottom heat for about 55 minutes. (350°F)

Fox Creek Cookie Cobbler

1 (16 oz.) can whole cranberry sauce
⅓ c. brown sugar
3 Tbsp. flour
1 tsp. cinnamon
4 apples, peeled, cored, sliced, and halved
½ roll of refrigerator sugar cookie dough

Blend together cranberry sauce, brown sugar, flour, and cinnamon in a large bowl; fold in apples and stir. Spread fruit filling into a 12-inch Dutch oven. Slice cookie dough into ¼-inch slices and lay over the filling. Cover and bake using top and bottom heat for 30–35 minutes or until apples are tender. (400°F)

Barrier Creek Apple Crisp

8 apples, peeled, cored,
and diced
⅓ c. orange juice
concentrate, thawed
⅓ c. sugar
1 tsp. cinnamon
1 c. flour
½ c. brown sugar
½ tsp. salt

Place apples in a greased 12-inch Dutch oven. Pour juice over top and sprinkle with sugar. Blend together cinnamon, flour, brown sugar, and salt. Sprinkle this mixture over apples. Cover and bake using top and bottom heat for 30 minutes or until topping is brown and apples are tender. (375°F)

Arrowhead Cranberry Apple Crisp

4½ c. peeled, cored, and
sliced apples
¾ c. whole cranberry
sauce
¾ c. flour
1 c. brown sugar
1 tsp. cinnamon
6 Tbsp. butter

Arrange apples in a greased 10-inch Dutch oven. Spread cranberry sauce on top. In a separate bowl, combine flour, brown sugar, and cinnamon. Cut in butter until crumbly. Sprinkle over apple mixture. Cover and bake using top and bottom heat for 35–40 minutes or until apples are tender. Serve warm or cold. (350°F)

Paradise Apple Crisp

6 baking apples, peeled,
    cored, and sliced
½ c. butter, melted
¾ c. brown sugar
¾ c. quick-cooking
    oatmeal
½ c. flour
½ tsp. cinnamon

Place apples into a greased 12-inch Dutch oven. Combine butter, brown sugar, oatmeal, flour, and cinnamon; sprinkle over apples. Cover and bake using top and bottom heat for about 35 minutes. (350°F)

All-Star Freedom Cobbler

1¼ c. flour
½ tsp. salt
½ c. shortening, chilled
    and cut into pieces
5–6 Tbsp. cold water
1 (10 oz.) pkg. frozen
    raspberries, thawed,
    juice reserved
¼ c. sugar
2 tsp. cornstarch
½ tsp. cinnamon
¼ tsp. nutmeg
2 apples, peeled, cored,
    and sliced

Stir together flour and salt; cut in shortening until mixture is crumbly. Add cold water 1 tablespoon at a time, until dough comes together. Wrap and chill for 1 hour. Place reserved raspberry juice into a 1-cup measuring cup and add enough water to equal 1 cup liquid. Combine sugar, cornstarch, cinnamon, and nutmeg in a saucepan; blend in raspberry liquid. Bring to a boil over medium heat, stirring constantly until mixture thickens. Remove from heat and stir in raspberries and apples. Pour cobbler filling into a greased, foil-lined 12-inch Dutch oven; set aside. Remove dough from refrigerator and roll out to ¼-inch thickness; cut with a star shaped cookie cutter. Place stars over fruit filling, overlapping if desired. Cover and bake using top and bottom heat for 25–30 minutes. (375°F)

Piñon Nut Apple Crisp

6 large apples, peeled,
    cored, and sliced
¼ c. diced piñon nuts
20 dates, softened and
    diced
1 c. apple juice
½ c. oil
¼ c. water
2 c. quick-cooking
    oatmeal
1 c. whole-wheat flour
½ tsp. salt

Place the apples, nuts, and dates in a 12-inch Dutch oven. Thoroughly mix the remaining ingredients together in a large bowl. Place mixture over apples and dates. Cover and bake using top and bottom heat for 45 minutes or until top is golden brown. Serve warm with ice cream. (350°F)

Apple Cinnamon Cobbler

4⅓ c. apples, thinly sliced
1½ c. sugar, divided
½ tsp. cinnamon
¾ c. chopped pecans,
    divided
1 c. flour
1 tsp. baking powder
½ tsp. salt
1 egg, beaten
½ c. evaporated milk
⅓ c. butter, melted

Arrange apple slices in an even layer in a greased 10-inch Dutch oven. In a small bowl, combine ½ cup sugar, cinnamon, and ½ cup pecans; sprinkle mixture over apples. In a separate bowl, combine flour, remaining sugar, baking powder, and salt; set aside. In a small bowl, whisk together egg, evaporated milk, and butter. Add to flour mixture all at once, stirring until smooth. Pour mixture over apples; sprinkle top with remaining pecans. Cover and bake using top and bottom heat for about 50 minutes. (325°F)

Broken Arrow Rhubarb Apple Cobbler

½ c. sugar

2 Tbsp. cornstarch

1 tsp. cinnamon

2 c. apples, peeled, cored, and chopped

2 c. chopped rhubarb

1 Tbsp. water

2 Tbsp. butter, melted

Topping

1 c. flour

½ c. sugar

2 tsp. baking powder

1 tsp. salt

⅓ c. milk

Combine sugar, cornstarch, cinnamon, apples, rhubarb, and water in a large saucepan. Cook over medium heat, stirring often until mixture boils. Boil for 1 minute and then pour into 12-inch Dutch oven. Drizzle melted butter over top.

To make topping, sift flour, sugar, baking powder, and salt together. Add milk and mix gently until only small lumps remain. Spoon topping over cobbler. Cover and bake using top and bottom heat for about 30 minutes. (400°F)

Brown's Hole Apple-Pineapple Crisp

⅔ c. sugar

1 Tbsp. cornstarch

1 tsp. grated lemon peel

¾ tsp. cinnamon

¼ tsp. nutmeg

4 c. tart apples, peeled and sliced

1 (20 oz.) can pineapple chunks, drained

¾ c. quick-cooking oatmeal

¼ c. flour

¼ c. brown sugar

⅓ c. butter, chilled

1 (3½ oz.) jar chopped macadamia nuts

In a large bowl, combine sugar, cornstarch, lemon peel, cinnamon, and nutmeg. Add apples and pineapple; toss to coat. Pour into a greased 12-inch Dutch oven. In separate bowl, combine oatmeal, flour, and brown sugar. Cut in butter until mixture resembles coarse crumbs. Stir in nuts; sprinkle over apple mixture. Cover and bake using top and bottom heat for 30 minutes or until topping is golden brown. Serve with ice cream or whipped topping. (375°F)

Fruit Cobbler with Oatmeal Biscuits

⅓ c. chopped dried
    apricots
¼ c. raisins
¾ c. apple juice
4 apples, peeled, cored,
    and thinly sliced
2 c. ripe pears, peeled,
    cored, and thinly
    sliced
2 tsp. lemon juice
¼ c. water
½ c. coarsely chopped
    walnuts

Topping
½ c. flour
½ c. oatmeal
2 Tbsp. sugar
1 tsp. baking powder
½ tsp. baking soda
½ tsp. salt
½ cube butter, chilled
    and cut into small
    pieces
½ c. plain, low-fat yogurt
    or buttermilk
cinnamon

Mix apricots, raisins, and juice in a 12-inch Dutch oven. Let stand for 30 minutes at room temperature. Add apples, pears, lemon juice, and water to oven. Cover and bake using top and bottom heat. Bring mixture to a boil over moderate heat. Reduce heat to moderately low and simmer 10–20 minutes or until fruit is tender. If mixture starts to dry, add more fruit juice and water. When fruit is firm but tender, stir in walnuts.

To make topping, mix flour, oatmeal, sugar, baking powder, baking soda, and salt in a large bowl. Cut in butter until mixture resembles coarse crumbs. Add yogurt or buttermilk and stir just enough to combine. Drop dough on top of fruit mixture in Dutch oven. Increase heat and bake, covered, for 20 minutes or until biscuits are golden brown. Sprinkle cinnamon on top. (425°F)

Hailstone Peach Cobbler

1 (16 oz.) can sliced
   peaches, undrained
1 c. flour
1¼ c. sugar, divided
1 c. milk
2 tsp. baking powder
⅛ tsp. salt
1 cube butter, melted

In a medium saucepan, bring peaches and juice to a boil over medium heat. In a medium bowl, mix flour, 1 cup sugar, milk, baking powder, and salt. Pour butter into 10-inch Dutch oven. Pour batter over butter. Add peaches; do not stir. Sprinkle remaining sugar over batter. Cover and bake using top and bottom heat for 20–30 minutes. Serve with ice cream or whipped topping. (400°F)

Mill Fork Peach Walnut Crisp

5 c. peeled and sliced
   peaches, fresh or
   frozen, thawed and
   drained
1 Tbsp. flour
3 Tbsp. sugar
½ c. quick-cooking
   oatmeal
¼ c. whole-wheat flour
2 Tbsp. wheat germ
½ c. brown sugar
¼ tsp. nutmeg
2 Tbsp. chopped walnuts
¼ c. buttermilk

Arrange peach slices in a greased 10-inch Dutch oven. In a small bowl, stir together flour and sugar. Sprinkle over peaches, tossing to coat. In a separate bowl, combine remaining ingredients except buttermilk; mix well. Pour buttermilk over oatmeal mixture and stir mixture with a fork until mixture resembles coarse crumbs. Sprinkle oatmeal mixture on top of peaches. Cover and bake using top and bottom heat for 30–35 minutes or until top is golden. (350°F)

Peach Blush Cobbler

3½ c. peeled and sliced
   peaches
1 Tbsp. lemon juice
1 c. sugar
½ tsp. salt
1 c. flour
1 egg, beaten
6 Tbsp. butter, melted

Place peaches in a lightly greased 10-inch Dutch oven; sprinkle with lemon juice. Stir; set aside. Sift together sugar, salt, and flour; add egg. Toss with a fork until mixture is crumbly; spread over peaches. Drizzle with butter. Cover and bake using top and bottom heat for 35–40 minutes. (375°F)

Juicy Peach Cobbler

1 cube butter, melted
1 c. sugar
1 c. evaporated milk
1 c. flour
1 Tbsp. baking powder
1 tsp. salt
1 (16 oz.) can sliced
   peaches, undrained

Place melted butter in a 12-inch Dutch oven; add sugar and milk and blend with a fork. Add flour, baking powder, and salt and mix just until smooth. Pour peaches and juice over top. Sprinkle with sugar. Cover and bake using top and bottom heat for 30 minutes or until crust is golden brown. Serve warm with ice cream. (350°F)

Summit Blueberry Raspberry Crunch

1 (21 oz.) can blueberry
    pie filling
1 (21 oz.) can raspberry
    pie filling
1 (18¼ oz.) box white
    cake mix
½ c. chopped walnuts
½ c. butter, melted

Combine pie fillings in a greased 12-inch Dutch oven. In a large bowl, combine cake mix, walnuts, and butter until crumbly; sprinkle over pie fillings. Cover and bake using top and bottom heat for 25–30 minutes or until filling is bubbly and topping is golden brown. Serve with ice cream or whipped topping. (375°F)

Ashley Valley Raspberry Crisp

4 c. fresh or frozen
    raspberries, divided
¾ c. sugar
2 Tbsp. cornstarch
1¾ c. quick-cooking
    oatmeal
1 c. flour
1 c. brown sugar
½ tsp. baking soda
½ c. butter, chilled

Crush 1 cup raspberries; add enough water to measure 1 cup. In a saucepan, combine sugar and cornstarch; stir in raspberry mixture. Bring to a boil; cook and stir for 2 minutes or until thickened. Remove from the heat and stir in remaining raspberries. Cool. In a large bowl, combine oatmeal, flour, brown sugar, and baking soda. Cut in butter until mixture resembles coarse crumbs. Pour cooled raspberries in a greased 10-inch Dutch oven, then sprinkle crumb mixture over filling. Cover and bake using top and bottom heat for 25–30 minutes or until top is lightly browned. Serve with ice cream or whipped topping. (350°F)

Lemon-Lime Raspberry Cobbler

2 (21 oz.) cans raspberry
   pie filling
1 (18¼ oz.) box white
   cake mix
1 (12 oz.) can lemon-lime
   soda

Pour pie filling into Dutch oven. Sprinkle dry cake mix over filling. Do not stir. Pour can of lemon-lime soda carefully and evenly over cake mix. Cover and bake using top and bottom heat for 20–25 minutes or until topping is crisp and fruit is hot and bubbly. (375°F)

Owlhoot Raspberry Cobbler

1 c. flour
¼ c. plus 2 Tbsp. sugar,
   divided
⅛ tsp. salt
1 cube butter, chilled and
   sliced into pieces
1½ Tbsp. cold water
2 (12 oz.) pkgs. frozen
   raspberries
2 Tbsp. whipping cream

Combine flour, 1 tablespoon sugar, and salt in a medium bowl. Cut in butter until mixture resembles coarse crumbs. Add water a few drops at a time, just enough to hold dough together. Place pastry on a lightly floured surface and roll into a circle about ⅛-inch thick and 14 inches in diameter. Fold and refrigerate about 20 minutes. Place raspberries in the bottom of a foil-lined 12-inch Dutch oven. Sprinkle evenly with ¼ cup sugar. Unfold dough and place over raspberries. Crimp edges with fork against side of oven; cut steam vents in dough. Brush with cream and sprinkle with remaining 1 tablespoon sugar. Cover and bake using top and bottom heat for 30–35 minutes or until pastry is golden brown and the fruit juices are bubbling in the center. Serve with cream. (375°F)

Bridger Creek Blueberry Crisp

1 (21 oz.) can blueberry
    pie filling
½ c. oatmeal
½ c. flour
¼ c. brown sugar
2 Tbsp. chopped walnuts
6 Tbsp. margarine

Spoon blueberry pie filling into a greased 10-inch Dutch oven. In a medium bowl, combine oatmeal, flour, brown sugar, and walnuts. Cut in margarine until mixture resembles coarse crumbs. Sprinkle over pie filling. Cover and bake using top and bottom heat for 45 minutes or until lightly browned and bubbly. (375°F)

Bonanza Blueberry Buckle

¾ c. sugar
¼ c. butter, softened
1 egg
½ c. milk
2 c. flour
2 tsp. baking powder
½ tsp. salt
2 c. fresh or frozen
    blueberries

Topping
½ c. sugar
¼ c. butter, softened
⅓ c. flour
½ tsp. cinnamon

Mix together sugar, butter, and egg; stir in milk. Stir together flour, baking powder, and salt; add to batter. Blend in blueberries. Spread batter into a greased 10-inch Dutch oven.

In a medium bowl, combine topping ingredients. Pour crumb topping over blueberry mixture. Cover and bake using top and bottom heat for 30–35 minutes. (375°F)

Blueberry Cobbler & Cinnamon Dumplings

1 (21 oz.) can blueberry
   pie filling
1 tsp. lemon zest
1 Tbsp. lemon juice
2 tsp. vanilla extract
1 (8 count) tube
   refrigerator
   cinnamon rolls
¼ c. chopped pecans,
   toasted
2 Tbsp. brown sugar

Combine first 4 ingredients in a lightly greased 10-inch Dutch oven. Cover and bake using top and bottom heat for about 10 minutes; remove from heat. Separate cinnamon rolls; set icing aside. Arrange rolls on top of fruit filling mixture; sprinkle with pecans and brown sugar. Cover and bake again using top and bottom heat for about 20 minutes. Drizzle with icing. (375°F)

Fisher Mesa Fruit Crumble

1 (10½ oz.) can apricot
   halves, drained
2 c. fresh or frozen
   blueberries
⅓ c. sugar
1 Tbsp. lemon juice
1 Tbsp. quick-cooking
   tapioca pudding mix
½ tsp. cinnamon
½ c. brown sugar
¼ c. flour
¼ c. oatmeal
½ tsp. cinnamon
¼ tsp. nutmeg
½ cube butter, chilled
   and cut into pieces
½ c. chopped walnuts
garnish: whipped topping

Blend together fruits, sugar, lemon juice, tapioca, and cinnamon. Place in greased, foil-lined 10-inch Dutch oven. In a large bowl, thoroughly mix brown sugar, flour, oatmeal, cinnamon, and nutmeg; cut in butter until mixture resembles coarse crumbs. Fold in nuts and sprinkle over filling in Dutch oven. Cover and bake using top and bottom heat for about 25 minutes. Cool slightly and garnish with whipped topping. (375°F)

Cherry Creek Crunch

1 (21 oz.) can cherry pie filling
1 (20 oz.) can crushed pineapple, undrained
1 (18¼ oz.) box yellow cake mix
1½ cubes butter, sliced
1 c. chopped pecans

Layer ingredients in order listed in a greased 12-inch Dutch oven. Cover and bake using top and bottom heat for 35–45 minutes or until golden brown. Serve warm. (350°F)

Carla's Cherry Cheesecake Cobbler

2 (21 oz.) cans cherry pie filling
2 (8 oz.) pkgs. cream cheese, softened
2 eggs
1 (14 oz.) can sweetened condensed milk
1 tsp. vanilla
1 cube butter, softened
1 c. flour
1 c. brown sugar

Pour cherry pie filling in a foil-lined Dutch oven. In a large bowl, beat cream cheese, eggs, condensed milk, and vanilla until smooth. Pour this mixture carefully over pie filling. Cover and cook with top and bottom heat about 25 minutes until cream cheese mixture is set. While this is cooking, mix butter, flour, and brown sugar until well mixed. Crumble this mixture over cooked cream cheese mixture. Cover and bake using top and bottom heat about 20 minutes until topping is somewhat crisp or lightly browned. (375°F)

Warm Springs Blackberry Cobbler

1 cube butter, melted
1 c. flour
1 c. milk
1½ c. sugar, divided
2 tsp. baking powder
2 Tbsp. cornstarch
2 tsp. lemon juice
½ tsp. nutmeg
¾ Tbsp. cinnamon
2 c. fresh or frozen
   blackberries

Pour melted butter into a 10-inch Dutch oven. Blend together flour, milk, 1 cup sugar, and baking powder; pour batter into Dutch oven. In a large bowl, mix together remaining ½ cup sugar and other ingredients and pour into center of batter in Dutch oven. Do not stir. Cover and bake using top and bottom heat for 35–45 minutes. Serve with your favorite cream topping. (375°F)

Six Shooter Blackberry Cobbler

8–10 c. fresh or frozen
   blackberries
¾ c. plus 3 Tbsp. sugar,
   divided
2 Tbsp. cornstarch
5 Tbsp. butter, melted
   and divided
2⅓ c. biscuit mix
⅔ c. milk

Place berries in a saucepan over medium-high heat, stir occasionally until berries begin to liquify. Mix ¾ cup sugar and cornstarch; combine with berries and stir until mixture comes to a boil. Add additional sugar to taste. Stir 2 tablespoons melted butter into berry mixture and pour into 12-inch Dutch oven. Combine remaining 3 tablespoons butter, 3 tablespoons sugar, biscuit mix, and milk. Drop biscuit mixture onto berries by the spoonful. Cover and bake using top and bottom heat for 20–30 minutes or until golden brown. (450°F)

Rhubarb Heaven

4 c. chopped rhubarb
1 c. sugar
1 (18¼ oz.) box white
    cake mix
1 (3 oz.) pkg. strawberry
    gelatin
1 c. water
⅓ c. butter, melted

Place rhubarb and sugar in a 12-inch Dutch oven; stir well. Sprinkle with dry cake mix, then gelatin. Pour water and butter over top. Do not stir. Cover and bake using top and bottom heat for 45–60 minutes. (350°F)

Upside Down Cranberry Crunch

3 c. fresh or frozen
    cranberries
½ c. chopped pecans
1¾ c. sugar, divided
2 eggs
½ c. butter, melted
1 c. flour

Place cranberries in a greased 10-inch Dutch oven. Sprinkle with pecans and ¾ cup sugar. In a large bowl, blend together eggs, butter, flour, and remaining sugar until smooth. Spread over cranberry mixture. Cover and bake using top and bottom heat for 1 hour or until a toothpick inserted near the center comes out clean. Run knife around edges of oven; immediately invert onto a serving plate. Serve with whipped topping or ice cream. (325°F)

Eureka Dewberry Cobbler

2½ c. dewberries
1 c. sugar
3 Tbsp. flour
3 Tbsp. butter
½ tsp. salt
¼ tsp. cinnamon
9-inch unbaked pie crust,
    torn into strips

In a large bowl, combine dewberries and remaining ingredients except pie crust; pour into a greased 10-inch Dutch oven. Cover dewberry mixture with pie crust strips. Cover and bake using top and bottom heat for 30 minutes or until pie crust is browned. (425°F)

Corral Canyon Dessert

1 egg, beaten
1 (8 oz.) can fruit
    cocktail, undrained
1 c. sugar
1 tsp. vanilla
1 c. flour
1 tsp. baking soda

Topping
1 c. brown sugar
½ c. chopped walnuts

In a large bowl, combine dough ingredients. Pour batter into a greased 12-inch Dutch oven.

To make topping, combine brown sugar and walnuts; sprinkle over top of batter. Cover and bake using top and bottom heat for about 45 minutes. Serve with dollops of whipped topping on top. (325°F)

Grizzly Bear Six-Fruit Crisp

1 (25 oz.) jar chunky
   applesauce
1 (20 oz.) can pineapple
   tidbits, drained and
   chopped
1 (15¼ oz.) can sliced
   peaches, drained and
   chopped
1 (15¼ oz.) can sliced
   pears, drained and
   chopped
1 (11 oz.) can mandarin
   oranges, drained
1 (21 oz.) can cherry pie
   filling

Topping

2 c. flour
2 c. brown sugar
1 c. butter, melted

Pour applesauce into a greased 12-inch Dutch oven. Layer with pineapple, peaches, pears, and mandarin oranges. Spread pie filling over top.

To make topping, combine flour, brown sugar, and butter. Sprinkle over pie filling. Cover and bake using top and bottom heat for 30–35 minutes or until topping is golden brown. Serve with ice cream or whipped topping. (375°F)

Fiery Furnace Sweet Potato Cobbler

2 lbs. sweet potatoes,
    peeled and sliced,
    ¼-inch thick
3½ c. water
1½ c. sugar
3 Tbsp. flour
½ tsp. cinnamon
¼ tsp. nutmeg
¼ tsp. salt
¾ c. butter, sliced

Pastry
2 c. flour
½ tsp. salt
⅔ c. shortening
5–6 Tbsp. cold water
2 Tbsp. butter, melted
4 tsp. sugar

In a saucepan, boil sweet potatoes in water until slightly tender, about 10 minutes. Drain, reserving 1½ cups cooking liquid. Layer potatoes in a greased 12-inch Dutch oven; add reserved liquid. Combine sugar, flour, cinnamon, nutmeg, and salt; sprinkle over potatoes. Dot with butter.

To make pastry, combine flour and salt; cut in shortening until mixture resembles coarse crumbs. Gradually add water, tossing with a fork; form into a ball. On a floured surface, roll pastry into a 12-inch circle. Place over filling; cut slits in top. Brush with butter; sprinkle with sugar. Cover and bake using top and bottom heat for 30–35 minutes or until top is golden brown. Serve with ice cream or whipped topping. (400°F)

Hobble Creek Pumpkin Crisp

1 (16 oz.) can pumpkin
1 (12 oz.) can evaporated
    milk
1 c. sugar
1 Tbsp. cinnamon
3 eggs
1 (18¼ oz.) box yellow
    cake mix
1½ c. chopped pecans
1 c. butter, melted
1 (8 oz.) pkg. cream
    cheese, softened
½ c. powdered sugar
1 c. whipped topping

Mix pumpkin, evaporated milk, sugar, cinnamon, and eggs together with a mixer until well blended. Pour into a greased, foil-lined 12-inch Dutch oven. Sprinkle dry cake mix over top, then sprinkle pecans over cake mix; drizzle butter over all. Do not stir. Cover and bake using top and bottom heat for about 1 hour. While crisp is cooling, blend together cream cheese, powdered sugar, and whipped topping and serve with cooled crisp. (350°F)

Sparkling Dump Cake

1 (21 oz.) can apple,
    cherry, or blueberry
    pie filling
1 (18¼ oz.) box yellow
    or white cake mix
1 (12 oz.) can lemon-lime
    soda

Pour pie filling in bottom of a greased 12-inch Dutch oven. Pour dry cake mix over top of pie filling. Pour soda evenly over pie filling and cake mix. Do not mix. Cover and bake using top and bottom heat for 47–52 minutes or until light golden brown. Serve warm with a scoop of vanilla ice cream or whipped topping. (350°F)

CAKES

Cakes are fun "try and see" desserts that are exceptional in Dutch ovens. Included here are a few traditional cakes, several pudding cakes, and some different upside-down cakes. Serve them up with ice cream, whipped topping, or just let them stand alone. They will surprise you!

Hummingbird Cake

3 c. flour
2 c. sugar
1 tsp. baking soda
1 tsp. salt
1½ c. oil
3 eggs
1 (8 oz.) can crushed
    pineapple, drained
2 c. mashed bananas
1 c. chopped walnuts

Sift together flour, sugar, baking soda, and salt; set aside. In a separate bowl, combine oil, eggs, pineapple, bananas, and nuts. Add flour mixture, mixing with a spoon. Pour batter into a greased 12-inch Dutch oven. Cover and bake using top and bottom heat for 1 hour or until toothpick inserted in center comes out clean. Serve with whipped topping or ice cream. (350°F)

Sunnyside Lemon Cake

1½ c. butter, softened
3 c. sugar
5 eggs
3 c. flour
¾ c. lemon-lime soda
2 Tbsp. lemon extract
1 tsp. lemon zest

Cream butter and sugar until light and fluffy; add eggs 1 at a time, blending well after each addition. Mix in flour, 1 cup at a time. Add lemon-lime soda, lemon extract, and lemon zest, mixing well. Pour into a greased and floured 12-inch Dutch oven. Cover and bake using top and bottom heat for 60–65 minutes or until toothpick inserted in the center comes out clean. Serve with ice cream or whipped topping. (350°F)

Promontory Applesauce Cake

⅓ c. shortening

1⅓ c. sugar

2 eggs

1 c. applesauce

⅓ c. water

1⅔ c. flour

¼ tsp. baking powder

1 tsp. baking soda

¾ tsp. salt

½ tsp. cinnamon

¼ tsp. ginger

½ tsp. cloves

⅓ c. chopped walnuts

Cream shortening and sugar; beat in eggs 1 at a time until mixture is light and fluffy. Add applesauce and water; set aside. In separate bowl, sift together flour, baking powder, baking soda, salt, cinnamon, ginger, and cloves; blend into applesauce mixture. Fold in nuts. Pour batter into greased 12-inch Dutch oven. Cover and bake using top and bottom heat for 1 hour or until toothpick inserted in center comes out clean. Serve with ice cream or whipped topping. (350°F)

Hideout Cake

3 c. flour

2 c. sugar

1 c. mayonnaise

⅓ c. milk

2 eggs

2 tsp. baking soda

2 tsp. cinnamon

½ tsp. nutmeg

½ tsp. salt

¼ tsp. cloves

3 c. peeled, cored, and
chopped apples

1 c. raisins

Combine first 10 ingredients; blend on low speed with a mixer for 2 minutes. Fold in apples and raisins. Pour batter into a greased 12-inch Dutch oven. Cover and bake using top and bottom heat for 45 minutes or until a toothpick inserted into the center comes out clean. Serve with ice cream or whipped topping. (350°F)

Jammin' Cougar Cake

¾ c. butter, softened
1 c. sugar
6 eggs
3 c. flour
1 tsp. baking soda
1 Tbsp. cinnamon
1 Tbsp. allspice
1 tsp. cloves
1 c. buttermilk
1¼ c. seedless blackberry
    jam

Cream butter and sugar in a large bowl. Blend in eggs 1 at a time; set aside. Combine flour, baking soda, and spices together; blend in sugar mixture alternately with buttermilk. Stir in blackberry jam. Pour batter in greased 12-inch Dutch oven. Cover and bake using top and bottom heat for 45 minutes or until a toothpick inserted in center comes out clean. Serve with ice cream or whipped topping. (350°F)

Washboard Snack Cake

2 c. flour
1 tsp. baking soda
2 tsp. cinnamon, divided
½ tsp. salt
⅔ c. shortening
1 c. brown sugar
2 eggs
1 tsp. vanilla
1 c. buttermilk
1 c. flaked coconut
½ tsp. nutmeg
¼ c. light cream

Sift together flour, baking soda, 1 teaspoon cinnamon, and salt; set aside. Cream shortening and brown sugar until light and fluffy. Blend in eggs 1 at a time, mixing well after each addition. Mix in vanilla; then mix in dry ingredients alternately with buttermilk. Spread batter into a greased 12-inch Dutch oven. Combine remaining ingredients; sprinkle over batter. Cover and bake using top and bottom heat for 35 minutes or until a toothpick inserted in center comes out clean. (350°F)

Indian Canyon Pear Cake

4 c. peeled, cored, and
    chopped pears
2 c. sugar
3 c. flour
1 tsp. salt
1½ tsp. baking soda
1 tsp. nutmeg
1 tsp. cinnamon
½ tsp. cloves
4 egg whites, beaten
⅔ c. oil

Combine pears and sugar in a large bowl; set aside for 1 hour. Mix flour, salt, baking soda, and spices together; set aside. Blend egg whites and oil into pear mixture; gradually blend in flour mixture. Pour batter into a lightly greased 10-inch Dutch oven; cover and bake using top and bottom heat for 60–70 minutes. (325°F)

Willow Plum Cake

¼ c. butter, softened
½ c. sugar
2 eggs
3 Tbsp. orange juice
1 c. flour
1 Tbsp. orange zest
¾ tsp. baking powder
½ tsp. nutmeg
1 lb. plums, quartered

Filling
1¼ c. sour cream
1 egg
2 Tbsp. orange juice
1 tsp. cornstarch

Streusel
1 c. flour
½ c. brown sugar
½ tsp. nutmeg
½ tsp. cinnamon
½ c. butter

Cream butter and sugar in a large bowl until light and fluffy. Mix in eggs and orange juice; set aside. Combine flour, orange zest, baking powder, and nutmeg; gradually blend into sugar mixture. Spread in a greased 10-inch Dutch oven; gently arrange plum quarters on top, skin-side up.

To make filling, blend ingredients until smooth and creamy. Spread filling gently over plums

To make streusel, combine first 4 ingredients; cut in butter using a pastry cutter until mixture resembles coarse crumbs. Sprinkle streusel over filling. Cover and bake using top and bottom heat for 60–70 minutes or until a toothpick inserted in the center comes out clean. (350°F)

Tamarack Blueberry Dump Cake

1 (15 oz.) can crushed
    pineapple
2 c. fresh or frozen
    blueberries
1 (18¼ oz.) box yellow
    cake mix
2 cubes butter, melted

In a greased 12-inch Dutch oven, layer pineapple, blueberries, and dry cake mix. Do not stir. Drizzle melted butter evenly over top. Cover and bake using top and bottom heat for 50 minutes or until golden brown. (350°F)

Pack Saddle Upside-Down Cake

¼ c. coarsely chopped
    walnuts
1 c. brown sugar
¼ c. plus 6 Tbsp.
    unsalted butter,
    divided
3 Tbsp. maple syrup
4 large ripe bananas,
    peeled and sliced
1 c. flour
2 tsp. baking powder
½ tsp. cinnamon
¼ tsp salt
¾ c. sugar
1 egg
½ tsp. vanilla
6 Tbsp. milk

Toast walnuts by placing them on a cookie sheet and baking for 5 minutes at 375°F; watch closely. Set aside to cool. Combine brown sugar and ¼ cup butter in heavy medium saucepan. Stir over low heat until butter melts and mixture is well blended. Pour into a 10-inch Dutch oven. Spread to coat bottom of pan. Pour maple syrup over sugar mixture. Sprinkle walnuts evenly over top. Place banana slices on nuts, overlapping slightly and covering bottom. In medium bowl, blend together flour, baking powder, cinnamon, and salt. Beat sugar and remaining butter in separate bowl until creamy. Add egg and vanilla; beat until light and fluffy. Beat in flour mixture alternately with milk. Spoon batter over bananas. Cover and bake using top and bottom heat for about 55 minutes. Carefully invert onto serving platter. Serve warm with whipped topping. (375°F)

Shingle Creek Carrot Cake

2 c. sugar
2 tsp. vanilla powder
½ c. chopped pecans
3 c. flour
2 tsp. baking soda
1 Tbsp. cinnamon
¼ tsp. nutmeg
⅛ tsp. cloves
1½ c. oil
3 eggs
3 c. grated carrots
1 (8 oz.) can crushed
    pineapple, undrained

Combine first 8 ingredients together in a large bowl; form a well in the center. Add oil, eggs, carrots, and pineapple; mix well. Pour into a greased 12-inch Dutch oven. Cover and bake using top and bottom heat for 40–50 minutes or until a toothpick inserted in the center comes out clean. (350°F)

Root Beer Cake

1 c. sugar
½ c. butter
½ tsp. vanilla
2 eggs
2 c. flour
1 Tbsp. baking powder
1 tsp. salt
⅔ c. root beer

Frosting

2 c. powdered sugar
1 c. root beer, chilled

Combine all ingredients in a large bowl. Blend at low speed; beat for 3 minutes at medium speed. Pour into greased 12-inch Dutch oven. Cover and bake using top and bottom heat for 30–35 minutes. (375°F)

To make frosting, combine powdered sugar and root beer in mixer bowl and blend well. Drizzle over each serving.

Raspberry Upside-Down Cake

1 (18¼ oz.) box yellow
   cake mix
1 c. raspberries
¾ c. sugar
½ c. whipping cream

Prepare cake mix according to package directions. Pour into a greased and floured 12-inch Dutch oven. Place raspberries over top of cake mix. Sprinkle sugar over raspberries. Gently pour whipping cream over top. Cover and bake using top and bottom heat for 25–35 minutes. Let stand for 10 minutes. Invert on plate to serve. (350°F)

Raspberry Almond Upside-Down Cake

¼ c. butter, melted
¾ c. sugar, divided
1½ c. fresh or frozen
   raspberries
2 Tbsp. sliced almonds
1½ c. biscuit mix
½ c. milk or water
½ tsp. vanilla
1 egg
2 Tbsp. oil
½ tsp. almond extract

Line a 10-inch Dutch oven with foil. Pour melted butter in bottom of Dutch oven; sprinkle evenly with ¼ cup sugar. Gently arrange raspberries over sugar mixture; sprinkle with almonds. In a medium bowl, beat remaining ingredients on low speed with a mixer for 30 seconds, scraping bowl constantly. Beat on medium speed for 4 minutes, scraping bowl occasionally. Pour batter over raspberries and almonds. Cover and bake using top and bottom heat for 35–40 minutes or until a knife inserted in center comes out clean. Immediately invert onto plate. Leave oven over cake for a few minutes so sugar mixture can drizzle over cake; remove from heat. Cool at least 10 minutes before serving. Serve warm with whipped topping. (350°F)

PUDDING CAKES

Pudding cakes consist of a layer of cake on the top and a layer of pudding on the bottom. The longer you bake it, the less pudding you get! Be sure *not* to stir cake batter after pouring on the final liquid.

Warm Springs Pudding Cake

2½ c. flour
1½ tsp. baking soda
1¼ tsp. ginger
1 tsp. cinnamon
½ tsp. salt
½ tsp. allspice
¼ tsp. nutmeg
½ c. sugar
¾ c. butter, softened and divided
1 egg
1 c. molasses
3 c. hot water
¾ c. brown sugar

Blend together flour, baking soda, ginger, cinnamon, salt, allspice, and nutmeg; set aside. Cream together sugar and ½ cup butter; beat in egg until well combined. Stir in flour mixture, adding alternately with molasses and 1 cup water. Pour into a greased 12-inch Dutch oven and sprinkle top with brown sugar. Combine remaining ¼ cup butter and 2 cups hot water, mixing well. Pour on top of batter; do not stir. Cover and bake using top and bottom heat for 40–45 minutes. Cake top will crack. Serve with ice cream or whipped topping. (350°F)

Castle Rock Cinnamon Pudding Cake

2 c. flour
1 c. sugar
2 tsp. baking powder
½ tsp. salt
3 tsp. cinnamon
1 c. milk
1¾ c. brown sugar
1½ c. water
2 Tbsp. butter
½ c. chopped walnuts
¾ c. peeled, cored, and chopped apples

Grease the bottom of a 10-inch Dutch oven. In a large bowl, mix together flour, sugar, baking powder, salt, and cinnamon. Make a well in the center and pour in milk. Mix well and pour into prepared oven. In a saucepan, combine brown sugar, water, and butter. Bring to a boil and pour over batter in the oven. Sprinkle top with nuts and apples. Cover and bake using top and bottom heat for 35–40 minutes or until a toothpick inserted into the center of the cake comes out clean. Serve warm. (350°F)

Gingerbread Pudding Cake

2½ c. flour
1½ tsp. baking soda
1¼ tsp. ginger
1 tsp. cinnamon
½ tsp. salt
½ tsp. allspice
¼ tsp nutmeg
½ c. butter, softened
½ c. sugar
1 egg
1 c. molasses
1 c. water
¾ c. brown sugar
1½ c. hot water
⅓ c. butter, melted

In medium bowl, combine first 7 ingredients; set aside. Beat softened butter and sugar in large bowl at medium speed until creamy. Add egg; continue beating until well mixed. Reduce speed to low. Alternately add flour mixture with molasses and water, beating after each addition until blended. Pour batter into 12-inch Dutch oven; sprinkle with brown sugar. Combine hot water and ⅓ cup melted butter in medium bowl; carefully pour over top of batter. Cover and bake using top and bottom heat for 40–55 minutes or until gingerbread is cracked on top and toothpick inserted in center comes out clean. Serve warm with ice cream. (350°F)

Tin Roof Sundae Pudding Cake

¾ c. flour
⅓ c. sugar
1 tsp. baking powder
¼ tsp. salt
½ c. milk
2 Tbsp. butter, melted
1 tsp. vanilla
⅓ c. chunky peanut
    butter

Chocolate Sauce
⅔ c. sugar
¼ c. cocoa
1¼ c. boiling water
¼ c. melted butter
vanilla ice cream
chopped peanuts

Mix flour, sugar, baking powder, and salt together in a medium bowl. Add milk, melted butter, and vanilla; stir until smooth. Stir in peanut butter. Pour batter into greased 10-inch Dutch oven.

To make sauce, mix together sugar and cocoa. Stir in boiling water until sugar is dissolved. Add melted butter. Pour mixture evenly over batter in oven. Cover and bake using top and bottom heat for 28–30 minutes or until toothpick inserted in center comes out clean. Let cool before serving. The chocolate sauce in the bottom of the oven will thicken as it cools. To serve, spoon chocolate sauce over the cake. Top with vanilla ice cream and chopped peanuts. (350°F)

Praline Pudding Cake

¾ c. dark brown sugar
1¼ c. plus 1 Tbsp. flour, divided
¾ c. sugar
⅓ c. chopped pecans
1 Tbsp. baking powder
¼ tsp. salt
½ c. milk
2 Tbsp. butter, melted
1½ tsp. vanilla
1¾ c. boiling water
2 c. whipped topping

Combine brown sugar and 1 tablespoon flour in a small bowl. In a large bowl, combine remaining 1¼ cups flour with sugar, pecans, baking powder, and salt; make a well in center of mixture. In a medium bowl, combine milk, butter, and vanilla; pour into the well in flour mixture. Stir just until moist. Spread batter into greased 10-inch Dutch oven; sprinkle with brown sugar mixture. Pour boiling water over batter; do not stir. Cover and bake using top and bottom heat for 35 minutes or until pudding is bubbly and cake springs back lightly in center. Serve warm with whipped topping. Garnish with pecans. (350°F)

Caramel Apple Pudding Cake

2 c. tart apples, peeled, cored, and thinly sliced (about 2 medium apples)
3 Tbsp. lemon juice
½ tsp. cinnamon
⅛ tsp. nutmeg
¼ c. raisins
1 c. flour
¾ c. brown sugar
1 tsp. baking powder
¼ tsp. baking soda
½ c. milk
3 Tbsp. butter, melted and divided
1 tsp. vanilla
½ c. chopped pecans or walnuts
¾ c. caramel flavored ice cream topping
½ c. water

Grease a 10-inch Dutch oven. Arrange apples in bottom of oven; sprinkle with lemon juice, cinnamon, and nutmeg. Top evenly with raisins; set aside. In a large bowl, stir together flour, brown sugar, baking powder, and baking soda. Add milk, 2 tablespoon melted butter, and vanilla; mix well. Stir in chopped nuts. Spread the batter evenly over the apple mixture. In a small saucepan, combine caramel topping, water, and 1 tablespoon butter; bring to boiling. Pour caramel mixture over batter in Dutch oven. Cover and bake using top and bottom heat for 35 minutes or until set in center. While warm, scoop onto dessert plates. Spoon the caramel-apple mixture from bottom of oven over each portion. Serve with whipped topping. (350°F)

Black Forest Pudding Cake

1¼ c. sugar, divided
1 c. flour
¼ c. plus 3 Tbsp. cocoa,
    divided
2 tsp. baking powder
¼ tsp. salt
½ c. milk
⅓ c. butter, melted
1½ tsp. vanilla
½ c. brown sugar
1¼ c. hot water
1 tsp. almond extract
1 (21 oz.) can cherry pie
    filling, warmed

Combine ¾ cup sugar, flour, 3 tablespoons cocoa, baking powder, and salt in large bowl. Add milk, melted butter, and vanilla; beat until smooth. Spread into greased 10-inch Dutch oven. Stir together remaining ½ cup sugar, brown sugar and ¼ cup cocoa in small bowl; sprinkle mixture evenly over batter. Combine hot water and almond extract; pour over batter. Do not stir. Cover and bake using top and bottom heat for 40 minutes or until center is almost set. Let stand 15 minutes. Spoon into dessert dishes, spooning sauce from bottom of oven over top. Serve with cherry pie filling.

Black Rock Brownie Pudding Cake

1 c. flour
⅔ c. cocoa, divided
¾ tsp. baking powder
¾ tsp. salt
2 eggs
1 c. sugar
6 Tbsp. butter, melted
     and cooled
½ c. milk
1 tsp. vanilla
½ c. chopped walnuts
¾ c. brown sugar
1⅓ c. boiling water

Sift together flour, ⅓ cup cocoa, baking powder, and salt. In separate bowl, whisk together eggs, sugar, butter, milk, and vanilla; add flour mixture and stir batter just until moist. Stir in walnuts and spread batter evenly in greased 10-inch Dutch oven. In separate bowl, whisk together remaining ⅓ cup cocoa, brown sugar, and water; pour mixture over batter. Cover and bake using top and bottom heat for 35–40 minutes or until a toothpick comes out with crumbs on it. Serve the cake hot with ice cream. (350°F)

Orangeville Pudding Cake

1 c. flour
⅓ c. sugar
1 tsp. baking powder
½ tsp. cinnamon
¼ tsp. salt
½ c. milk
2 Tbsp. butter, melted
½ c. chopped pecans or
　　walnuts
¼ c. currants or raisins

Sauce
⅔ c. brown sugar
¾ c. orange juice
¾ c. water
1 Tbsp. butter
1 tsp. orange zest

In a large bowl, combine flour, sugar, baking powder, cinnamon, and salt. Stir in milk and melted butter until combined. Stir in nuts and currants or raisins; spread batter in greased 10-inch Dutch oven.

In a small saucepan, combine sauce ingredients and bring to a boil over moderate heat, stirring occasionally. Boil for 2 minutes and carefully pour sauce over batter. Cover and bake using top and bottom heat for 30–40 minutes. Serve with creamy topping. (350°F)

Sweet Chocolate Pudding Cake

1 c. flour
2¼ c. sugar, divided
½ c. cocoa
2 tsp. baking powder
¼ tsp. salt
¾ c. milk
¼ c. butter, divided
1 tsp. vanilla
1½ c. water

Preheat 10-inch Dutch oven for 15 minutes. In a large bowl, sift together flour, ¾ cup sugar, cocoa, baking powder, and salt. Add milk, 3 tablespoons butter, and vanilla, stirring until smooth; set aside. Combine remaining sugar and water in a small saucepan. Bring to a boil, stirring to dissolve sugar. Remove from heat. Place remaining 1 tablespoon melted butter in preheated oven and coat well. Add batter, spreading evenly in oven. Pour water mixture over batter; do not stir. Mixture will bubble. Cover and bake using top and bottom heat for 28–30 minutes or until cake is set. Let stand 10 minutes before serving. (375°F)

Chocolate Fudge Pudding Cake

¾ c. sugar
1 Tbsp. margarine
½ c. milk
1 c. flour
2 tsp. baking powder
¼ tsp. salt
2 Tbsp. cocoa

Topping
½ c. sugar
½ c. brown sugar
⅓ c. cocoa
1½ c. boiling water

Mix all cake ingredients well and spread in a greased 10-inch Dutch oven.

To make topping, mix sugar, brown sugar, and cocoa and sprinkle over batter in oven. Slowly and evenly pour boiling water on top. Do not stir. Cover and bake using top and bottom heat for 35–40 minutes. Serve warm with whipped topping or ice cream. (350°F)

Whole-Wheat Rhubarb Pudding Cake

5 c. sliced rhubarb
2½ c. sugar, divided
1¼ c. flour
½ c. whole-wheat flour
1 c. chopped pecans
1¼ tsp. baking powder
½ tsp. cinnamon
¼ tsp. nutmeg
¼ tsp. salt
¾ c. milk
¼ c. butter, melted
1 Tbsp. cornstarch
1¼ c. boiling water

In a 12-inch Dutch oven, mix rhubarb and ¼ cup sugar. In separate bowl, mix flours, 1 cup sugar, pecans, baking powder, cinnamon, nutmeg, and salt. Stir in milk and melted butter. Spread batter evenly over rhubarb-sugar mixture. Mix remaining 1¼ cups sugar and cornstarch. Add boiling water; stir until sugar dissolves. Slowly pour over the batter. Cover and bake using top and bottom heat for 45 minutes or until a toothpick inserted in center of crust comes out clean. Serve with creamy topping. (375°F)

Horseshoe Cinnamon Pudding Cake

1 c. sugar
2 Tbsp. butter
1 c. milk
2 c. flour
2 tsp. baking powder
2 tsp. cinnamon

Topping
2 c. brown sugar
2 Tbsp. butter
1¼ c. water

Mix all cake ingredients together and blend well. Pour into a greased 12-inch Dutch oven.

To make topping, combine ingredients in a saucepan; bring to a boil. Pour mixture over cake batter. Do not stir. Cover and bake using top and bottom heat for about 25 minutes. (350°F)

Blueberry Pudding Cake

2 c. fresh or frozen
    blueberries
2 Tbsp. lemon juice
1 c. flour
2 tsp. baking powder
¼ tsp. salt
½ tsp. nutmeg
1¾ c. sugar, divided
½ c. milk
1 egg
¼ c. butter, melted
1 tsp. vanilla
1 Tbsp. cornstarch
1 c. boiling water

Place blueberries and lemon juice in greased 10-inch Dutch oven. In a medium bowl, mix together flour, baking powder, salt, nutmeg, and ¾ cup sugar. Beat in milk, egg, melted butter, and vanilla. Spread over berries. Mix remaining 1 cup sugar with cornstarch and sprinkle over batter. Pour boiling water over all; do not stir. Cover and bake using top and bottom heat for 40–50 minutes.

Caramel Nut Pudding Cake

½ c. sugar
1 Tbsp. butter
1 tsp. vanilla
½ c. milk
1 c. flour
½ tsp. nutmeg
½ tsp. baking soda
pinch of salt
½ c. chopped walnuts

Sauce

1 c. brown sugar
2 Tbsp. butter
2 c. boiling water

In a large bowl, cream sugar and butter together; add vanilla. Then add milk, flour, nutmeg, baking soda, and salt. Mix to make a smooth batter; add nuts. Pour into a greased 10-inch Dutch oven.

To make sauce, combine sauce ingredients and pour over top of cake batter. Do not stir. Cover and bake using top and bottom heat for about 25 minutes. Serve with ice cream or whipped topping. (375°F)

PUDDINGS

Have you ever tried making bread pudding in a Dutch oven? Well, next time you want to make something different, try a pudding. Included in this section are several recipes for bread pudding and some good old-fashioned rice pudding. Not as common in a Dutch oven, but just as good.

Elkhorn Raisin Bread Pudding

1 (1 lb.) loaf white bread, cubed
6 c. milk
5 eggs, beaten
1 Tbsp. cinnamon
1½ c. brown sugar
1 c. raisins
cinnamon and sugar to taste

Sauce
1 c. sugar
2 Tbsp. cornstarch
2 c. boiling water
2 tsp. vanilla
4 Tbsp. butter

Place bread in a greased 12-inch Dutch oven. In a large bowl, blend together milk, eggs, cinnamon, brown sugar, and raisins. Mix well and pour over bread; sprinkle with cinnamon and sugar. Cover and bake using top and bottom heat for 1½–2 hours or until golden brown. (350°F)

To make sauce, combine sugar and cornstarch in a saucepan. Gradually stir in boiling water; continue boiling for 1 minute, stirring constantly. Add vanilla and butter; stir until butter is melted. Pour over pudding.

Topaz Lemony Bread Pudding

2 c. dry bread, cubed
4 c. milk, scalded
1 Tbsp. butter
¼ tsp. salt
¾ c. sugar
4 eggs, beaten
1 tsp. vanilla

Topping
¾ c. sugar
1 Tbsp. cornstarch
⅛ tsp. salt
⅛ tsp. nutmeg
1 c. boiling water
2 Tbsp. butter
1½ Tbsp. lemon juice

Soak bread in hot milk for 5 minutes. Add butter, salt, and sugar. In separate bowl, beat eggs, then pour bread mixture over eggs. Add vanilla and mix well. Spoon into a greased 10-inch Dutch oven. Cover and bake using top and bottom heat for 50 minutes or until firm. (350°F)

Mix sugar, cornstarch, salt, and nutmeg; gradually add water while stirring. Cook over low heat until thick and clear. Add butter and lemon juice; blend thoroughly. Serve over bread pudding.

Prickly Pear Bread Pudding

1 tsp. rum or orange
   extract
1 tsp. water
½ c. raisins
1 Tbsp. butter
2 c. pears, peeled and
   sliced
½ c. sugar, divided
4 c. white bread, cubed
3 c. milk, scalded
3 eggs, beaten
1 tsp. vanilla
1 c. whipping cream

In a small saucepan, blend together rum or orange extract and water. Heat just to boiling and pour over raisins. Melt butter in saucepan; stir in pear slices and sauté for 5 minutes. Stir in ¼ cup sugar and continue to cook for 2 minutes. Place bread in a greased 10-inch Dutch oven, pour in milk and let soak 5 minutes. Fold in raisin and pear mixtures. Thoroughly combine eggs, remaining sugar, vanilla, and cream; combine with bread mixture. Cover and bake using top and bottom heat for about 50 minutes. (350°F)

Cinnamon Bread Pudding

6 eggs
2 c. milk
2 c. half-and-half, divided
1 c. sugar
2 tsp. vanilla
6 c. cinnamon bread,
   cubed
½ c. brown sugar
¼ c. butter
½ c. corn syrup

In a large bowl, whisk eggs; blend in milk, 1¾ cups half-and-half, sugar, and vanilla until combined. Stir in bread cubes until lightly moistened. Grease a 12-inch Dutch oven and spread mixture evenly. Cover and bake using top and bottom heat for 55–60 minutes or until center starts to firm. In small saucepan, heat brown sugar and butter until butter is melted. Carefully, add corn syrup and remaining half-and-half. Cook, stirring constantly over medium heat, for 1–2 minutes or until sugar dissolves and mixture is smooth. Serve over warm pudding. (325°F)

Cinnamon Raisin Bread Pudding

12 c. cubed cinnamon
    bread
1 c. raisins
1 tsp. cinnamon
6 eggs, beaten
6 c. milk
1 c. sugar

Sauce
4 Tbsp. butter, melted
2 tsp. vanilla
1 c. boiling water
1 c. sugar
2 Tbsp. cornstarch

Place bread cubes in a greased 12-inch Dutch oven; sprinkle with raisins and cinnamon. In a separate bowl, combine eggs, milk, and sugar; blend well. Pour over bread. Press bread down with a fork until bread is soaked. Cover and bake using top and bottom heat for 1 hour or until set.

Place butter and vanilla in a saucepan with boiling water. Mix sugar and cornstarch together and add to liquid mixture. Cook over low heat until semi-thick, stirring frequently. Pour sauce over cooked pudding. (350°F)

Ghost Rock Bread Pudding

3 c. cubed bread
3 eggs, beaten
3 c. warm water
1 (14 oz.) can sweetened
    condensed milk
2 Tbsp. butter, melted
1 Tbsp. vanilla
½ tsp. salt
cinnamon and sugar to
    taste

Place bread cubes in greased 10-inch Dutch oven; set aside. In a large bowl, combine all remaining ingredients; pour evenly over bread. Sprinkle with cinnamon and sugar. Cover and bake using top and bottom heat for 45–50 minutes. (350°F)

Lodge Pole Bread Pudding

3 eggs
3 c. milk, scalded
⅓ c. plus 2 Tbsp. sugar, divided
5 bread slices, cubed
⅓ c. raisins
2 tsp. cinnamon
lemon pie filling

In a large bowl, beat eggs; add milk and mix well. Stir in ⅓ cup sugar, bread cubes, and raisins. Pour mixture into greased 10-inch Dutch oven. In a small bowl, combine remaining sugar and cinnamon; sprinkle over top. Cover and bake using top and bottom heat for 30–40 minutes. Serve with heated lemon pie filling. (350°F)

Calico Chocolate Bread Pudding

4 bread slices, cubed
1 oz. unsweetened chocolate, chopped
4 c. milk
2 eggs, beaten
1 c. sugar
1 tsp. vanilla

Place bread cubes in a medium saucepan. Stir in chocolate and milk and bring to a boil, stirring constantly. Remove from heat. Blend eggs and sugar together and gradually pour milk mixture over egg-sugar mixture, constantly stirring. Mix in vanilla and pour into a greased 10-inch Dutch oven. Cover and bake using top and bottom heat for 1 hour or until knife inserted in center comes out clean. (350°F)

White Mesa Bread Pudding

1 loaf french bread, cubed
1 (16 oz.) can sliced peaches, drained
½ c. raisins
4 eggs, beaten
¾ c. sugar
1 (12 oz.) can evaporated milk
2 c. milk
½ tsp. cinnamon
¼ tsp. nutmeg
1 tsp. coconut extract
1 Tbsp. vanilla

Place bread cubes, peach slices, and raisins in a greased 12-inch Dutch oven; stir gently and set aside. Combine eggs with sugar. Stir together evaporated milk, milk, spices, coconut and vanilla extracts, and egg mixture; blend. Pour this mixture evenly over bread, gently stirring to coat completely. Cover and bake using top and bottom heat for 30–40 minutes or until a knife inserted in center comes out clean. (350°F)

Silver Reef Bread Pudding

6 bread slices, cubed and divided
2 Red Delicious apples, peeled, cored, coarsely chopped, and divided
3 Tbsp. raisins
¼ c. chopped walnuts
2 eggs, beaten
⅔ c. sugar
2 Tbsp. butter, melted
1½ c. whipping cream
1 c. apple juice
½ tsp. cinnamon
½ tsp. nutmeg

Place half of the bread cubes in bottom of a greased 12-inch Dutch oven, then layer with half of the apples. Top with remaining bread cubes. Toss together raisins and walnuts and sprinkle over bread layer. Top with remaining apples. Blend eggs, sugar, and butter; stir in cream, apple juice, cinnamon, and nutmeg. Pour over top of bread mixture; do not stir. Cover and bake using top and bottom heat for 40–50 minutes or until a knife inserted in center comes out clean. (350°F)

Pine Creek Pineapple Pudding

½ c. butter, melted
5 bread slices, cubed
3 eggs, beaten
3 Tbsp. flour
½ tsp. salt
¾ c. sugar
1 (20 oz.) can crushed
    pineapple, undrained

Place butter in a large skillet, add bread cubes and sauté until golden; set aside. Place eggs in a large bowl, add flour, salt, sugar, and pineapple; mix well. Pour this mixture into a greased 10-inch Dutch oven. Add bread cubes, pushing bread down into pineapple mixture. Cover and bake using top and bottom heat for 35–40 minutes. (350°F)

Boulder Bread Pudding

3 eggs, beaten
1 (12 oz.) can sweetened
    condensed milk
3 apples, peeled, cored,
    and chopped
1¾ c. hot water
¼ c. butter, melted
1 tsp. cinnamon
1 tsp. vanilla
4 c. french bread, cubed
½ c. raisins

In a large bowl, combine eggs, condensed milk, apples, water, butter, cinnamon, and vanilla. Stir in bread and raisins, completely moistening bread. Pour into a greased 10-inch Dutch oven. Cover and bake using top and bottom heat for about 1 hour. Serve with whipped topping. (350°F)

White Chocolate Berry Bread Pudding

4½ c. biscuit mix
3½ c. milk, divided
¾ c. grated white
   chocolate
2 Tbsp. butter, softened
4 eggs
1⅓ c. milk
⅔ c. sugar
1½ c. heavy whipping
   cream
1 Tbsp. vanilla
1 c. frozen raspberries
1 c. frozen blueberries

Berry Sauce
⅓ c. sugar
2 Tbsp. biscuit mix
1 c. frozen raspberries
1 c. frozen blueberries
½ c. water

In a large bowl, stir together biscuit mix and 1⅓ cup milk. Drop dough by heaping tablespoons onto large ungreased cookie sheet. Bake in a 450°F oven for 8–10 minutes or until golden brown. Cool on wire rack about 30 minutes. Break up biscuits into random pieces; spread into a greased 12-inch Dutch oven. Sprinkle with grated white chocolate. Beat remaining ingredients except berries and berry sauce in large bowl using mixer on low speed until blended. Pour over biscuits in Dutch oven. Cover and refrigerate for at least 8 hours but no longer than 24 hours. To bake, stir raspberries and blueberries into biscuit mixture. Cover and bake using top and bottom heat for 1 hour or until knife inserted in center comes out clean. (350°F)

To make sauce, stir together sugar and biscuit mix in a saucepan. Stir in remaining ingredients. Cook over medium heat until mixture thickens and boils, stirring constantly. Boil and stir 1 minute; remove from heat. Pour warm berry sauce over pudding and serve.

Kolob Creek Bread Pudding

4 c. bread cubes
⅔ c. milk
2 eggs, beaten
2 Tbsp. butter, melted
1½ c. applesauce
¼ c. brown sugar
1 tsp. cinnamon
½ c. raisins
lemon pie filling

Combine ingredients except lemon filling in order given and place in a greased 10-inch Dutch oven. Cover and bake using top and bottom heat for 45–60 minutes. Serve with heated lemon pie filling. (350°F)

Notch Canyon Bread Pudding

2½ c. bread cubes
2½ c. milk
4 Tbsp. butter
½ c. honey
½ tsp. salt
2 eggs, beaten
1 tsp. vanilla
½ c. raisins
½ c. chocolate chips

Place bread cubes in a large bowl. Heat milk to a boil and then pour over bread. Let stand for 5 minutes. Add butter, honey, and salt; mix well. Let cool for several minutes. Mix in eggs, vanilla, raisins, and chocolate chips. Pour mixture into a greased 12-inch Dutch oven. Cover and bake using top and bottom heat for 1 hour or until a knife inserted in center comes out clean. (350°F)

Miner's Basin Rice Pudding

1 c. cooked rice
½ c. sugar
3 eggs, beaten
1 tsp. vanilla
1 (12 oz.) can evaporated
  milk
¼–½ c. golden raisins
¼ c. butter, chilled and
  sliced

Place warm rice in a large bowl. Add sugar, eggs, and vanilla. Pour evaporated milk into a 4-cup measuring cup and add enough water to make 4 cups of liquid. Add to rice mixture; blend in raisins. Pour rice mixture into a greased 10-inch Dutch oven; dot with butter slices. Cover and bake using top and bottom heat for 30–35 minutes. Serve warm. (350°F)

Hole-in-the-Rock Rice Pudding

4 Tbsp. rice
4 c. milk
dash of salt
½ c. sugar
2 tsp. grated orange peel
1 c. chopped dried fruit

In a large bowl, combine all ingredients, except dried fruit, and place in a greased 10-inch Dutch oven. Cover and bake using top and bottom heat for about 2 hours. About 30 minutes before it is done, stir in desired amount of chopped dried fruit. (300°F)

Split Mountain Rice Pudding

½ c. plus 2 Tbsp. long
    grain rice
4 c. milk
2 Tbsp. sugar
2 Tbsp. butter, melted
1 tsp. vanilla
nutmeg

Sauce
2 Tbsp. butter
¾ c. brown sugar
2 Tbsp. water

Place rice in a greased 10-inch Dutch oven. Combine milk, sugar, melted butter, and vanilla. Pour this mixture over rice and stir well. Sprinkle with nutmeg. Cover and bake using top and bottom heat for 2–2½ hours. Check often to prevent over cooking. Serve with sauce. (300°F)

To make sauce, melt butter in a small saucepan; add brown sugar and water. Cook until sugar is dissolved. Serve over pudding.

Henry's Fork Rice Pudding

2 c. cooked rice
¼ c. raisins
1 c. crushed pineapple,
    undrained
¾ c. hot water
1 tsp. vanilla
½ tsp. almond extract
3 Tbsp. orange juice
    concentrate
1 medium banana

In a greased 10-inch Dutch oven, mix together rice, raisins, and pineapple. In separate bowl, blend remaining ingredients until smooth and creamy. Pour blended ingredients over rice mixture and stir. Cover and bake using top and bottom heat for about 30 minutes. Serve warm. (350°F)

Pumpkin Rice Pudding

2 c. rice
6 c. milk
1 c. sugar
1 tsp. vanilla
1 tsp. grated orange peel
¼ c. orange juice
¼ tsp. salt
1 c. canned pumpkin
¼ c. brown sugar

In a greased 10-inch Dutch oven, combine rice, milk, sugar, vanilla, orange peel, orange juice, and salt. Cover and bake using top and bottom heat for 20–25 minutes. Check to prevent over cooking. When done, stir in pumpkin. Sprinkle with brown sugar to serve. (350°F)

Cascade Springs Chocolate Rice Pudding

4 c. cooked rice
¾ c. brown sugar
¼ c. cocoa
3 Tbsp. butter, melted
1 tsp. vanilla
2 (12 oz.) cans
    evaporated milk
1 c. slivered almonds

In a greased 12-inch Dutch oven, combine all ingredients. Cover and bake using top and bottom heat for about 2 hours. Check to prevent over cooking. (350°F)

INDEX

ABOUT THE AUTHOR

Carla Randolph loves to cook comfort food for her family and friends. She enjoys the outdoors, camping, hunting, and fishing. She also loves decorating her home and yard for the holidays. Carla is Mother to three married sons and Nana to six grandchildren. She lives in northern Utah with her husband, Phil.